THE
FACT
OF
THE
MATTER

Also by Sally Keith

Dwelling Song
Design

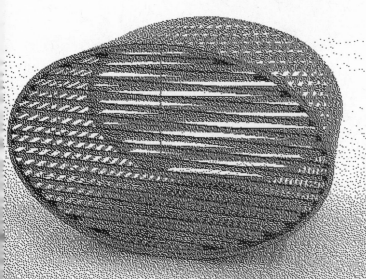

THE FACT OF THE MATTER

SALLY KEITH

POEMS

milkweed editions

(800) 520-6455

www.milkweed.org

Published 2012 by Milkweed Editions

Printed in Canada

Cover design by Hopkins/Baumann

Cover art by Jane South, image courtesy of the artist and Spencer Brownstone Gallery, New York

Interior design by Hopkins/Baumann

The text of this book is set in Bodoni Book.

12 13 14 15 16   5 4 3 2 1

First Edition

Please turn to the back of this book for a list of the sustaining funders of Milkweed Editions.

Library of Congress Cataloging-in-Publication Data

Keith, Sally.
   The fact of the matter : poems / Sally Keith. -- 1st ed.
      p. cm.
   ISBN 978-1-57131-448-2 (alk. paper)
   I. Title.
   PS3561.E3773F33 2012
   811'.54--dc23

                              2012019997

This book is printed on acid-free paper.

for my mother

*

Contents

Revelation has no dimensions.

—Robert Smithson

THE
FACT
OF
THE
MATTER

PROVIDENCE

The restaurant owner opened the doors
to let in the smell from the sea
which stuck on the breeze. On the table,
a white linen, a low candle, a tiger lily bouquet.
The specials chalked in cursive we read
from a slate, while the waiter, starched shirt
and folded apron, explained them and we ordered,
at first, a carafe of a thinner than usual pale colored wine.
My mother sat across from me.
She did not lean into her elbow on the table, did not
slide her weight up her arm to make a leading shoulder.
The light in her eyes was first a pool, then a line.
Outside the skiffs in exit sailed toward us.
On the corner a crushed Diet Coke can.
What she then told me, I remember.
Salt was exploding all over the sea.

STUDY IN INCREMENT

One conversation is contained in the room.
Two women, but only one chair to comfortably sit in.
Light falls.

*

Add that one is in love with the other.
It might have been you.
Outside, the slovenly light falling on and through the shape of the sycamore leaf,

*

siphoned, somewhat deflected where the vascular connectives knot, but soft, is so.
It is dusk.
Pinks and red.

*

If somewhere Achilles is soaking in the still hot Mediterranean sun,
elsewhere I study the pieces of a painting.
One woman is standing.

*

The woman standing beside the well glances inward at a sylvan conversation.
There is a shepherd.
There is a man with red bouffant sleeves and a cap.

*

This painting is Bellini's.
It hangs in the National Gallery four miles away from the room where I write.
Mine was the conversation.

*

To understand the quality of resistance tightening, take Agamemnon annoyed.
Achilles is soaking.
He dangles his hand down from the hammock, hot sun, into the hair of the other.

*

Counter to natural inclination, the collage artist, my friend, has cut the canvas in half,
reattached it leaving a gap, which makes the scene more real.
For dusk, a coppery auburn color.

*

The red hints show real anger.
If you lift the ancient Athenian vase and stare,
in gold, encircled there: two figures and around the outside a procession.

*

To step from the path of a person approaching is so different from dodging a thing.
The body in time, a body absorbing.
Outside the slatted walnut-tree leaves are discernible against the sky,

*

whereas on the grass they fall without precision.
There is a shepherd with bare feet.
There is a man with an embroidered shirt who carries a flute.

*

The two are conversing.
The one with the flute looks in at the conversation.
The one pouring water looks into the well, bored and unrelenting.

*

Think of Achilles.
Achilles does not want to bury his friend because he loves him.
In the room, that one will wrong the other is the inevitable situation.

*

But Achilles will not bury Patroclus's body until the ghost arrives and commands him.
I understand.
He wants another moment to touch him.

*

Instantaneousness though is the proof of nothing.
The one pouring water looks bored by the others.
According to X-radiography, once she had not been.

*

Inside the room there is a pattern.
Longer then shorter gaps punctuate the increasingly lively postconcert conversation.
It was my friend who explained to me the vase as she saw it in a museum.

*

Achilles uses both of his hands to tend to his friend's wounded arm.
The tendon in Patroclus's outstretched foot parallel to the backs of the men
is the force holding the image inside the frame.

*

They want to stay.
The pupils of their eyes are very wide, admissive of pain, but so pleased there,
perfect in that, the stillness there is before the epic moves again.

WEDDING OF THE RAILS

To make the model escape was a kind of moral imperative.
Due to technology one can go back, reread the conversation.

I am ambivalent. Ambivalence connotes parallel emotions. Ambi-
as in on both sides, as in ambiciliate or ambidextrous. To be ambivalent is not

the fault of the body but rather a natural condition. But why devise a model
of the self when models don't make anything happen? Force started the study

not ambivalence, which was a kind of result. Force is that which changes
the moment of rest or alters the motion of a body in a line.

A Greek mathematician under the moon gathered the facts from the sea.
In the brief visitor center film, force moved our nation into modernity.

I need some force to deal with time. It was 1869. They found it strange
to watch the men pounding an iron ladder into the ground.

When I ask the woman for a beer, she takes my wrist and leads me in
but the store is actually a wall full of watches and now I have to have one.

She takes them down, one at a time, stretching the straps around my wrist
each time unable to close them. I only want a beer, I say, I only want one.

Finally, I'm dreaming again. The reenactment of the railroad joining happens
twice each hour all day. Leland Stanford was the Union Pacific tycoon.

Eadweard Muybridge had been famous for photographing mountains.
Leland Stanford made a bet regarding the legs of a horse when it runs.

That the sentence hold the thinking self intact may require a strong defense.
Ignominious decision when the other side just quit, my father wrote me

yesterday, describing a case he had been working on. Each sentence predicts
a rhyming moment a countable distance away in time: hawthorn, jetty,

railroad, dome. Pattern of pelicans when three new birds join the migratory train.
Old letters, a sack of stone, sound of the answering machine saying no one is home.

Crystal in a staircase shape or crystal on a string: the growth of crystals out from
dislocation fascinated the artist Robert Smithson. *I am ambivalent.*

Don't cry. Because we have records of everything, you can go back, re-parse
the conversation. The flight of the horse is actually a line. Force is "that X."

And so mapping the course of the body along a grid on the wall, background
brightened by lime on the ground, Muybridge recorded the action for Stanford.

Emotion begins in two neurons like almonds in the brain. To find the force of the gait
labs use force plates in motion kinetics labs. Don't worry. Don't cry.

Force is "that X that turns anybody subjected into a thing." You know what they say
about time. The body of a horse shines. The hair of a horse is sharp on the hands.

Employees at the National Park Service perform the reenactment wearing uniforms.
If my voice sounds far away, I apologize: cell phones. "For every action there is always

an equal reaction," wrote Newton. The final tie pounded in. We celebrate it: gold.
I am ambivalent. Snow on the peak outside is white. Snow the color of the sky.

SCOUT

The woman explains how the child just sat,
    his father now gone. It wasn't their fault, but
the hair was wrong. He had always worn a buzz cut.
        Who is there supposed to be out in front of such a force?
For example, a soldier is sent to make a search,
    or plain sunlight on the flattened side of a New England house.
The regular talks nonstop.
        Jesus was a scout: vanguard, outrider, listener, a lookout.
Beside the two women, three men in Hawaiian shirts sit.
    If you ask me, to pay attention would be my best advice.
A new field but I remember tiny poppies among the wheat.
        That the other woman had lost a daughter is the information
withheld until now. "Looking at the Overlooked,"
    reads the brochure's boldfaced subtopic, just above
Chop Suey, 1929, two women in cloche hats and tight shirts.
        Pages flip. The regular talks. The lipstick was okay,
she before had noted, for adding the necessary life.
    The crepe myrtle blooming. The cranes disappeared.
This is the strip mall where my mother used to shop.

REREADING

Beyond the epic,
time spreads out into
space. Beyond
the thin dark gaps
between shapes the stars hold
and their mostly imperceptible
drift, the supernatural is
the extraordinary point

reached. The epic—
that is the one Thoreau says
Alexander carried
with him on expeditions
in a precious casket—
opens on anger. Anger
motivating force
by which a line unfurls,

event feeding on event,
specifically is supernatural
according to the Greek.
A gift from his teacher
Aristotle, this
so-called casket
copy, Alexander slept
on top of along with

a dagger. Each night
on a box, he for whom
the horizon was not
impossible—
ocean, mountain, desert, lake—
but to be surpassed
slept. Box
the body is caught

too tightly inside—
inversely the ocean,
so free, is not
to be found unlike anger
for slowly it swells
and should not be doubted
in its often invisible
force. One might even

admire it: the ocean,
marvelous less
because of the waves'
monotonous motion, or
any other character
of composition, color
or shape, but for the sense
inherent in endlessness.

One travels to the edge
to see what always is.
The wind blows hard.
The wind blows harder.
Achilles is angry.
The Greek men are waiting
by the emptied ships,
their horses chewing

large clumps of clover
and parsley. The wind
hits at hard angles
blowing up from the valley
where, flat, the orchards
and vineyards panel
the land at large. Orchard
branches leafless in winter

commingle and thatch,
so that it looks as if
a pool of smoke seeps,
rising faintly up
where the hilltop village
sits. The distant walls,
one long façade, a line
both as present and absent

to the onlooker, as I am
to myself. *There was a world,
or was it all a dream* is Helen.
Cedar branches later
and locks of hair for covering
the body down
into the earth. The wind
is a front. The wind

slams the shutters up
against the front of the house
though the strength of it
stays in the chimney, boxed
an inexhaustible breath—
raging, a kind of
violence. It's white.
Mid-days' flat light is

blanching the land,
spreading out. The earth
feels kept this year in winter
longer. Wild doves
and hollowed ships
repeat. In Keats's final
poem it is the hand
in the icy silence of

the tomb that is super-
natural as in the capacity
it takes on, so he makes
us feel, to haunt.
It is so bad not to remember.
Hector takes off his helmet,
horsehair-crested, to be
sure to be recognized

by his baby son. In 1621
Johannes Kepler
switches out "soul"
for "force." The bodies
of the horses keep glistening.
Cattle are described with over-
sized heads. Raging,
Achilles must go on

making decisions. Why
so vividly might I remember
standing on a ridge
above an icy river—
but inside the museum
no sense at all of the figures
though I remember them there
as bright? A barge cut

the ice leaving an arc
of black in its wake. Black
in the wool of the coats,
looking back at the photographs,
contrasts with the tarp there
wrapping the saplings
into ghostly white shapes.
Love—

I know we feel the world
too much. Facing downward,
the hand on top of the other
rests empty except for
the branches lining the palm.
The hand inside the hand
is a ghost. The wind,
wild doves, and hollow ships

repeat. Now,
except for the occasional
dried grape-skin still
stuck to the vine,
long after harvesting
the vineyards are bare.
Achilles too well knows
his fate. Curled

the oak leaves keep
attached to the branches
despite the strength of the wind.
Because Hector has chosen
Achilles' armor,
taken from the body of
the beloved
now gone, Achilles

knows also the vulnerable
points, the opening
at the back of the neck
exposing the skin.
Any spiral's math
implying forward motion
is a fact, still to believe
one ever stays in a single place

is the strange necessity
of concentration,
· I remember thinking.
I remember thinking:
here I am
watching my grandfather
in rural Tidewater, Virginia
eating Chinese. The waiter

has greeted us with a frame,
photograph of his newborn son.
My grandfather is lifting
fried pieces of meat
from his plate one by one.
I had spent the afternoon
alone, watching the river
where herons happened

to dive and sea gulls hovered
in predictable formations.
It might have been yesterday.
The field ploughed the third
time, the grapes harvested,
the party ongoing, the ocean,
a wedding, the court, and war:
engraved in gold these are

the images spiraling the shield,
the one world spun into the other,
the shield requested by the mother
for the son. At the moment
Hector is killed we read
his wife is weaving. Imagine—
the wind is blowing harder.
There is a swallow tracing

the limit of the bare oak
branches, its movement works
as if an invisible force
triggered some sporadic
shot-back mechanism of
the wings—shape of
the tiniest boat, a motion
mimicking the sea.

KNOT

The spine is a series of knots in a line.

The spine is made of bone and holds the body up.

Gravity pulls down.

"Knots made humans human" reads the newspaper this morning,

noting dressmakers, the suture, and the first stone axe.

The spine is the series where action begins.

When I woke up this morning the bank was covered again in snow.

Already April and bluebells under the box elder, tulips on the hotel's manicured slope.

Dreaming of water falling in lines and drowning the earth,

Albrecht Dürer woke up and started painting.

Dürer after three months of marriage took leave from his wife for Italy.

The spine is a series of knots under skin.

The spine is twenty-four knots if you start from the neck and work down.

If you pull back the curtain, you can watch a warrior in action—

Ajax picks up the wrong stone and steps up to face his enemy, Hector.

The winner will be rewarded the armor, but the body—

they promise the body will go back home.

Can you hear a sound in the back of your head urging against this?

Go home, go home.

Blood stains all systems in the body an equal red, explains Leonardo:

"You can have no knowledge of one without confusing and destroying the other."

Nearby Dürer paints on linen.

Dürer cuts a block of wood to print *The Sixth Knot* on Italian paper,

refashioning the ornate engraving from Leonardo's academy.

So one vision forces another.

"Imagine stacking the vertebrae, one on top of the other, and roll yourself up,"

says the yoga instructor, standing beside the window, the window a sheet shot with light.

Outside it is colder than usual.

I feel my own weight when I walk down the street.

I watch the red of a cardinal on a sky that is otherwise white.

Imagine the 20th of May, 1515.

On a ship full of species the rhinoceros arrives in Portugal, a gift for the king.

It had been over one thousand years since anyone in Europe had seen one.

When Dürer found out, he began his woodcut imagining—

put a gorget at the throat, rivets along the seams, and covered the spine in armor.

Soon it become a symbol: "I shall not return without victory."

And how many times shall we need it?

Can you hear a sound in the back of your head urging against this?

What wild grace it was when the rhino, forced to face the elephant

in order for the boastful king to test the account of Pliny, fled the arena.

Mostly we are vulnerable.

CRANE

I.

We finish our drinks on the balcony, looking out.
A band of artificial light separates city and sky.

The wind has stopped. This is how night works.

We do not imagine the club room inside,
not the fake portraits, the pool table, or the bar.

The building across from us is all cross sections.
Inside the silver girders, bare lightbulbs burn.

We wonder more about wiring than the dirt on the floor.
Eight steel boxes hang. Otherwise, night is neat enough.

The crane arms all aim in the same direction.
From far away it looks as though we lean.

II.

A table cuts the shadow exactly in half.
The man with earphones in a notebook writes.

Because the beer truck stops in the fire lane,
the drugstore owner runs out to the curb and screams

as a dirt bike leans,
the sidewalk three squares deep.

"At least strive for glee," says someone else.

The banner is flat against the crane's long arm,
against the jib that carries the trolley as it runs.

Blue latticework adds new angles to the sky.
On the chrome of the fenders, white stars burn.

III.

Supple enough for springing on fish, the bent heron neck
looks ancient, like driftwood. When the hurricane hit

the water ran up, flooded the point, floating parked cars.
Now the water is slow, a plank leaning in at the land.

We leave for lunch and after lunch the fig tree, the locust
and the old persimmon. This is how we grew up—

the southern maple in the boxwood, ivy matted under the porch.
"Distract me" is an unfair request.

At dusk the animals slip back onto dark tracks they've cut in the trees.
Come morning, the men arrive to lift the houses onto stilts.

Remaindered is the wind.

WHAT IS NOTHING BUT A PICTURE

I.

I could not make him come to me. A dozen times
the fresco dried before I made the face, the face
I'd kiss, my father, standing in the middle
of the marsh, the wind slung low at his feet,
one pink hand against his hip.

We'd met again in early spring. Dead trees rose
like sticks where eventually owls would nest.
The flowers were purple tufts.
The flowers struck us like props.
We were there and not there all at once.

Red swans were gliding in random patterns
knocking their plumage against
one another and occasionally dipping their beaks,
breaking the viscous sheen.

We'd gone beneath the leaves so that the rain
never got to us. We knew how it felt—
this feeling before a dream,
knowing a thing we could never touch.

II.

Above the mural the skyline measured only an inch.
In the foreground I was painting an onion dome,
craning my neck, dozing in and out of sleep.

I heard a far-off voice: "Do not trust in the horse."
Or was it: house? "Onion, omen. Omen, onion,"
floated up and out of the loamy earth.

Below only the gardener's Red Emperors in a row.
Only an iron mobile made of sharp-jawed fish,
hung above me heavy on the Wednesday sky.

Occasionally a high-pitched creak. Soon, though,
the afternoon storm beat out dusk. "This is the way
I know you will leave me," I heard in the early gust.

III.

Just past six and saffron threads tick
    in the ruddy angles of incoming light
increasing in width as they cross the waves,
       slow, steady, and otherwise black.
On the board where I stand to paint
    one curled frond rests by my foot.
My lantern light is now past pale
       but still I'm stuck on the intricate work
of the bees, wing-nets, their tiny feet
    folded up for flight, circling, circling
the laurel tree. And yet as ominous
       as they once were? I have my doubts.
The watchdogs rest in their holes.
    On the beach below, my friend is wading
out into the oncoming tide. He stops.
       He turns a blue bucket around at his waist
as he scoops up eels which, later, we'll eat.

IV.

On the silky grass behind the yard-wide cattail strip
while swallows dart, while the same heron keeps bending its knee—

in front of the hills we've wandered in already,
I'll paint this wall a mural to remind us of the past.

For rest: one small cot.
For fourteen hours a day: just green.

Despite the sea on which I'd arrived,
field was the only place I knew.

To paint this meant daubing the paint,
sweeping away the milkweed dander.

The men who settled there with me watched.
They hummed as I worked.

On the thin white papers of cigarette trash
they handed me up their written requests.

V.

I never sent a single note. It was March.
We were forward going or so it felt.

The ice on the river long melted
and unusually subdued were the dips

where the eddies stirred. On the surface
dulled depressions shone. Swollen fingerprints.

Make something, I thought—
but the brown river just sat

and was not worth following yet.
Sleep kept the work enough apart.

It was spring. I was to be married
as soon as I made it back. Cells multiplied

on the branch tips, all crevice-rife and lull.
Below the scaffolding, tulip bulbs swelled.

The white petals brushed up by the wind
kept on reminding me.

VI.

Three ships tick to an eerie swelling of bells,
three Nordic ships. It was a fleet
of fat toys afloat at the end of the world—

edges all overlapping so that as long as we watched,
heads propped up over the promenade wall—
even sleeping I knew . . .

it was the part in the mural where tall ships
approach and the mast tips must inch, one past
the other, so as to look real in stealing inland.

I had painted thin grass blades tangled
in courtyard stone. For tiny petals on moss beds
I chose the same periwinkle shade as for the sliver
of moon. Dolphins cut the tide in the distance.

But here the paint blends so the masts'
dark shade runs into the sky and sea.
Everything feels effortful.

The light was blinding and I stood.
Wheaten and indigo, all day the color
I'd dreamed of the sea stayed with me.

VII.

Our history was not at all unusual:
intruders versus natives and the hero
whose fate it is to find a new home.

Bored by the battle scene and dreading
the work, I tried a new technique. My men
were quick, spreading the resinous pitch
on the plaster so that later my oils would stick.

Later we'd light a fire while the wall dried,
eat eels from the morning catch, and dance.

I'd obsessed over all the old systems
for us versus them, for arranging the heads
and the horses of the combatants, spaced
diagonally by the lines of their shafts.

I had to think fast: lines of horses and men,
men and horses and behind them lightning
to crack the dark sky. I started slowly.

Where one man sits eating his soup,
I painted a gun in across his knee.

VIII.

One moonbeam bounced. Light
on the helmet of the boy was all
it took to betray him—far left side

of the scene—under night, otherwise
thick with shadows, otherwise ink
all over the forest's mossy floor.

He'd gone to help but first had begged
the men to tell his mother if . . .
and so to comfort her when he was gone.

Buckets full of tulip petals
stored in the far corner of the shed
for the funeral march, much later.

On the right side of the scene—
the heavy fingers of the mother
still hot from her loom as she cries

for her son, as she curses herself
for forgetting the cloth she had woven
to cover him down into the earth.

It was all so obvious.

IX.

My mother wrote to tell me disease
took the oak outside the back door.
The snowdrops this morning were new.

She's gathered the branches, scraped
and found them not light, not light
enough, at least, so she is waiting

for me to return. She will keep them.
I do the work I must. I paint the soldiers
planting branches around the bodies

and from these they hang helmets,
breastplates and swords. Then light
from that silver catches the sun, turns

and gleams. There is not a song
soft enough. There is nothing—
neither mullein, nor wool, nor snow—

soft enough that we know. My mother
is waiting with the branches, cool, wrapped
in wax paper, and she will keep them.

X.

My men climbed up
to get at the sound
they thought was an errant
wind working. High up
against the scaffolding,
the pitch of whining tin.
There I was.
Their eyes went everywhere.
Their long teeth shone
in the sun. I said I would
stay, hoping they'd go.
But the impasse only
extended as I showed
the ochre flowers
smoldering the far-off knoll,
the fish in the narrow
river shining, the mountain
fragments inserted around
the battle scene. Behind us
the pale sky pressured
the sea's much longer run.

XI.

The battle scene should be cleared
    of bodies blocking the field. Help will
have to be hired in taking the stump
    down to the ground. What do you call
the problem of losing words on the way
    to your throat? They'll have to hire men
to grind the stump, wait for the roots
    to disintegrate, malnourished then, for
the roots to turn into earth, for the loam
    to let the roots back in. Where is the quill,
the lantern, the desk of oak? I just put on
    pants and a shirt in the morning,
just raise my feet when it feels right to walk,
    open my mouth and hope for words. Soon
men will be hired to help with the stump. Wind
    will press on the small of my back as I work
fitting bodies back in the earth. I promise you
    somehow I'll get home, just wait—

XII.

In the afternoons my profile stretches.
The wind so full of ocean salt it stings.

My men insist upon siesta,
leaving me here alone.

I speak loudly out into the empty coast,
practicing the marriage toasts they'll make me.

I mimic shipwreck, gesturing wildly
each time I catch the slightest shadow from an arm.

I hold my cupped palm high up, away from me
and imagine the pulse of my love, imagine—

my speech would be so eloquent if not for the gulls,
if not for the wind cornered there in the reeds.

I have the body of a king.
My chest still puffs when I think of it.

XIII.

In the ultramarine my men had crushed
    from lapis lazuli, I finished the sheen
edging the long blades of the swords
    as they hung from the branches,
as they blew in breeze on the field
    where the battle had been, where
now I put daisies, cowslip, and heather.
    It was best here alone in the afternoon.
I kept the clouds small, low, and distinct.
    I edged them in black
with the pressed grapevine dye
    we had used earlier in the morning
to lay out the scenes. To the middle I mixed
    an almost blue drop, hoping
to hint at a chance from the past, to lead
    to the joy in the last banquet scene.
I should have sent a note, it's true.
    It wasn't that it was better here
studying sugar beets
    to get at the shade of the sky
at dusk, but there was something
    I was that wouldn't give up.

XIV.

I titled it "In Memory Of" and everybody knew.
I'd studied most the path away from fact, the line of men
heading downhill, leaving what they'd hoped was home.

From here dark elbows against the sun—
an ant line's narrow track along the cliff.
White flowers in patches of moss, dark sea roots.

They walked hauling sacks. The circular moon rose.
Wind hit their faces in fat swells. On the far side of the delta
the harbor holding their fleet. Inches under the water,

color of gun sheen, color of grass, a school of bony fish
swept, unknown to them. My marriage would be an error.
Everybody knew. Still we passed the time with wondering

into how many shapes a body could go.

XV.

"Don't touch them. They are dirty!" is the sound
of a sister repeating what she remembers
from her mother to the younger one whom now
she feels privileged to watch over,
who now stoops down to reach for the feather
beside the smaller pebbles, pieces of seaweed,
and driftwood scraps where once the water had been.

Soon the sound of the waves overwhelms them.
I turn toward the hills. The mural is almost done.
And if, sad, ever you've had to finish a job,
if even to imagine methods of finishing, then you know.
It is fine to be mesmerized, to count, repeatedly,
the time it takes one wave to move from full height
to the far-off point where foam soaks
into the sand, then leaves—

XVI.

The greyhounds lope at dusk.
Their bones shine. The leaves on the blue trees,
aluminum brittle, shook foil for the sea below
where loosed ship joints clutter and swell.
Around the sea-blackened boards
packets of seed have been spilled on the waves.
Above this scene my mother is the angel
teasing me from her place at the top of the trees.
Patches of wind toss the hard grass
so my shins get scratched.
The dogs' hot breath hits in gusts.
Clouds thicken. Clouds splice
down far-off mountainsides no one sees.
The surface of the ocean is heavy.
The surface is a ruin that breathes.
Still, the circumference of my arms
isn't yet wide enough. Mother,
don't haunt me: I'm still so far from home.

THE FACT OF THE MATTER

Industry sprang up.
Orange flowers surrounded the metallic poles.
The statue was a painted hawk with outstretched wings.
Sun beams spread out on wall-sized panes.
Two knights in armor were shown on the door.
People believed in me when I opened my coat.
An origami cat.
The poem a great gray wall.
The wall the softest kind of sheet.
Cosmos clustered in the median strip.
Soft pink slowed the city's strong wind.
The cosmos' stems shone electric green.
Elsewhere out flew a couple of cranes.
A beautiful boy into the velvet curtains pressed.
The stage is the barest black.
The hills behind it backlit, gold-rimmed.
A woman steps out and opens her hand.
Why do you weep? I ask.
She only unfurls her fingers to offer some seed.
She only bends her knees.
The world is the same. The world is the same.
The long green reeds will remain.
The wind inside is softly carving its name.

ON FAULT

I've not imagined well enough the composition of the earth,
I confess.
As for the air around the falcon's wings in flight,
I have considered it.
I've watched the falcon dive, its soundless fall
from the long bands of volcanic cliffs.
Lower down, porous lichen sheets peel from cypress.

"Are you Catholic?" is a common question people ask
of others they figure feel too much guilt.
Fault is defined as a flaw inherent to the self,
if not the responsibility for an accident.
But *is it* your fault
when whatever it was couldn't be helped or
when the outcome looking back is better than you first expect?

A fault is an extended break in a body of rock.
"I've had this house too long to watch it fall,"
is the man's objection to the drilling
the seismic response to which
one cannot predict.
"Blemish" suggests a fault of the body. Although fault implies
failing, failure is much more serious.

"I did not intend for it to work like this."
"It may resolve itself, I hope."
"I just cannot anticipate."
"Fractures well cured make us more strong,"
is George Herbert's advice, easy enough to hear in retrospect,
for example, having recently fallen and injured myself—
but not so for the one whose house in the hills on fracture rests.

I want to see how an underground river pressured
upward is heated to steam. "I'm sorry,
the next tour takes place in three months."
Here is the nation's largest producer of geothermal power.
Up in the hills you can see the cooling towers work.
Inside the visitor center: a Make-Your-Own-Earthquake machine.
Just jump on the ground and watch the pen shake.

"Believe, intend, expect, anticipate, and plan
are all forward-looking phrases," reads the information sheet.
I hate feeling wary of the things people say.
In the play *King Lear,* Lear is on the stage,
on the heath asking that the thunder
"Strike flat the thick rotundity of the world"—
a plea that is impossible, of course, but metaphorically it works.

Around the earth's inner core a fluid outer core circulates
affecting the earth's magnetic force. Every 500,000 years
it shifts. To say one thing in terms of another
connotes both metaphor and myth.
"We do cause quakes," is the straight-up admission
of the employee at the plant.
"I hope" is one thing; "I had hoped" quite another.

I saw an orange-red wildflower on the path. I saw a yellow bush.
The pattern of eruptions from California's Old Faithful
some call a predictor of quakes, though the science is mysterious.
Surrounded by bamboo and pampas grass, tourists sit and watch.
Mount Saint Helena is the backdrop.
That night at the bar when I ordered a glass he brought me a flight.
He did it twice.

"I'm sorry," she said.
"I'm sorry" is the phrase from my vocabulary I'm trying to strike.
Millions of gallons of treated water are pumped from Santa Rosa County.
Fissured rock, a water source, and volcanic earth—
a geothermal plant's three basic requirements.
That magnetism is on the decrease is one fact.
That Lake County has the cleanest air in all of California is another.

See: Troy Thompson, Lake Malawi in Africa, and characteristics
of lava-eating fish to learn Old Faithful's healing legend,
posted there on a plaque. It wasn't his fault.
But he wasn't allowed to do it. Was he sorry? I don't know.
Ash from volcanoes is used to make Comet and Ajax.
Volcanic ash is the best-kept secret
for mud baths, say the world's elite beauty spas.

"You are cautioned that any such forward-looking statements
are not guarantees for future performances"
is from the statement's final paragraph.
I spent three nights in Calistoga,
just south of Robert Louis Stevenson State Park.
I never had the mud bath.
I just didn't want it. I'm like that.

"It may be that Lear is asking for a storm
less than he is actually describing it," surmises the actor
when the director suggests he play Shakespeare coolly
regardless of the fact that Lear is hot.
"Don't bash it, breathe it,"
is how the director explains realizing the text
without layering on the emotional self.

In fact, if you remove the glass from the windows
in Europe's oldest cathedrals, you'll find them thicker at the base,
a fact proving the viscosity of glass.
Because the concrete box culvert is a barrier
for the Steelhead Trout making the seventy-mile trip
from the Russian River to upper regions of Big Sulfur Creek,
the company adds a chute and ladder to help.

"Do you know how many phone calls come in the summer
reporting what appear to be fires in these hills,
but really are the cooling towers at work?" she asks
offhandedly flipping through the binder-thick printout,
record of all the local quakes.
Have you seen the Russian River where it empties at the coast?
Green-soaked and lush, the lowland almost rocks.

It was spring when I made the trip.
To look and look, mist in exit, clouds separate, so light falls
through a slat casting a bright line on the flat of the sea
is the kind of looking that you cannot pull back.
Two guys surf. An unusual green colored rock.
To be sorry to have not yet had lunch, as far as guilt goes,
does not count, but remember the rule before that.

For eccentricities, "foible" or "shortcoming"
is better than "fault."
The way I understand it, diamonds just shoot
upward from the core of the earth.
Faults are a natural characteristic—
to have done so many things so wrong already—
to have not done anything so very wrong yet—

FOR EXAMPLE

The pale undersides of sycamore leaves, knocking
at seed pods hanging in brown bunches

so that they helicopter down.
Slag heap, mad slack, taut song:

Which morning am I making up now?
Somewhere wild animals are seeking cool hollows

in which to lay themselves down.
A wall of cotton disperses in the wind.

INLAND MIGRATION

Only once have I driven home through a fire,
but twice have I sat by the carousel in Avignon
dumbly amused by the children wanting
or not the pleasure of turning, not a one of them
unable to decide. It is true,
extinct are the moa and elephant birds
but still representing the ratites, the emu,
kiwi, rhea, and ostrich, large birds
with oversize breastbones that once
were graced with flight but are no more.

Named after the Swiss geologist, Agassiz,
and covering over the heart of the then continent
America, this giant glacier, glacier
which according to the scientists melted
within the span of a year, brought
with it manifold great myths of the flood. Man
arrives, final mountains rise. Inland migration
brings the usefulness of caves, arrow-
heads, and with the urn the idea
of wanting. It strikes me that in places

most often thought of and most loved
to whence return can almost lack meaning, there is
a kind of being that is an erasure. From the story
of Noah and the dove, etcetera,
comes the idea horizon, the green branch,
the wavering. Do you remember
the lemon drink that afternoon as tasting
bitter, or not? That there was no fire that time,
that there is none, but time, concerns me
as I fear we are burning as
the children turning wave goodbye.

THE ACTION OF A MAN

*

He shot the man who took his wife.
Muybridge did.
Whiskey, whiskey & smoke, smoke—
outermost edge of the burning, burning sun—
what does one do at the end of the day

to soothe oneself? From the museum
seventeen miles to the ancient lake,
home to sea monkeys, brine shrimp &
bacteria that blooms. Of the Pleistocene—
the lake once covered up

entire states. From any direction
the sculpture is spiral in shape.
And how many tons of stone did it take?
How many boxes breaking up light?
Mud, salt crystals, rocks, water . . .

North, North by East, Northeast by North . . .
Weaving large baskets out of reeds
sent for from San Francisco
the Cantonese, as in the deep Yangtze
Canyons, lowered themselves down

to blow out the rock. For the train itself,
for its speed, for steam, for the movement
of steam rising off, early motion photographers
held understandable intrigue.
To see that exhibit take the elevator down

four flights, go out the front door,
turn right two times and cross the bridge.
It was an economy class rental, an Aveo,
entirely white. It was instantaneous:
he shot him dead who took his wife.

*

I was there that day without a phone.
From blood comes blow & bloom,
etymologically. The wind blew.
The water was said to be red. The wind
sounded loudest from the bluff where I sat

blowing inside the pelican wings, air
sifting stone. Unfulfilled
was Asa Whitney's lifelong dream
to see the tracks span the coasts.
Occidental the famous horse's name

Muybridge photographed for Stanford.
To get to the gallery the bridge
you have to cross is called the Taft,
Northwest, Washington, DC.
To get shellac, to coat the coils

sketched on the record, for the gramophone,
first you had to find the bug:
you punctured the bug to get the dye.
Shellac as slang, is to beat or thrash.
The work was unusually dangerous

requiring the men to tamp black powder
into the holes, shallow in the rock face,
find a light for the fuse despite
the strong wind. "Celestials"
they called the Cantonese

because of the other world in which
they believed. Where does one go
to eat around here? At the end of the day
what does one do to soothe oneself?
I would have called. That much I know.

*

The edges of the lake don't seem to move.
This was my first observation, apart from
the sculpture, Smithson's, the *Jetty*
pressed down into the salt, the crystals
of salt framing the shape. "Lake"

according to Dürer was the best for red.
According to Chesterton *Red is the most joyful*
and dreadful thing in the physical universe . . .
He took whatever kind of transportation
he could get: wagon, train, or else, a boat.

He shot him dead. Whiskey & smoke.
Whiskey for the railroad gangs, smoke
signals in the distant hills, threads of
smoke rising from the cigarettes.
The directions I sent you are from my house.

Mud, salt crystals, rocks, water . . .
South, South by West, Southwest . . .
The mountains look as though they broke.
The black shadow casts across the flat
of the earth, convincing me, again

motion starts somewhere else. It wasn't
that the waterfall most interested him
(Muybridge) but the steam, movement
of steam rising off. You can see it
in his photographs, a tesseract.

Shrubs hold up at right angles.
A yellow bird is dead in the fresh oil slick.
I just thought somehow we would keep in touch.
Etymologically, lake once referred to linen
& crimson, lake as in to leach, to like.

*

Says the voice in the film circling the sculpture
Mud, salt crystals, rocks, water . . .
Southwest by West, West by South, West . . .
Press your thumb into the sea.
Drop the rock in the palm of your hand.

Cubes of salt have attached to the black basalt.
Saltbush, Fivehorn, Smotherweed, Little Sagebrush.
The man shouts to his wife across the lake—
salt crusting the surface lets you walk out on top of it—
there are mice living in the oil drum, all rusted out.

(I don't know whether to believe him or not.)
Beside the jetty, an abandoned mining camp.
I should have brought the phone.
What kind of walls are there, holding together
the parts of the heart? How many spirals

hide inside the brain as we know it *wider than*
the sky? The horizon shakes as the camera pans.
This place reminds me of the moon.
Mud, salt crystals, rocks, water . . .
On the doorknob he must not notice his hand.

The hand stretches out through the open space.
In the opening of the doors, the hand centers itself.
To the chest of the other, the hand aligns,
to the heart. He got the news and couldn't stop.
Evaporation

is the only way for a pluvial lake
to escape. "You burn me"
is Anne Carson's translation of Sappho
Fragment #38. I didn't know what was next.
My idea of sculpture says Carl Andre *is a road.*

*

The name of the bridge is the Taft.
The largest concrete bridge in the world
in 1907: a miracle of compression &
exceedingly rare, designed by
the famous railroad bridge engineer

George S. Morison. From 55,000
cubic yards of concrete, left to cure
on the ground below for a year, seven
Roman arches have been hoisted up,
filled in with tiers of airy spandrels.

That a horse lifts all four of its hooves
in full gallop was the achievement
of the photograph. I first saw it,
Smithson's *Spiral Jetty,* a tiny fern head
pressed down into a crimson wash,

in the series of aerial photographs.
David Maisel shot them from a helicopter.
From a helicopter (helix for spiral in Greek)
Smithson who had finished the *Jetty,*
having arranged for dump trucks to haul

the heavy basalt, who had marked
the diagonal line of the spiral
with a string, lost his life
in Texas surveying a prospective
site. I would have called.

I cannot stop myself from thinking this.
The pace of the car is painfully slow.
I worry the washed-out gravel road
will give me a flat. It is pink at dusk.
I cross the bridge returning home.

*

Connecting the coast, to see the tracks
was Whitney's lifelong dream. It was
James Howden, the British chemist, who
made better the blowing out of rock for tracks.
With nitroglycerin less oil was needed.

It expedited work by half. Even the clearing
of smoke was quick. After the trial and not
acquitted, Muybridge left. There is no possible
frame-by-frame explanation. Mountains,
the Modoc Indian War, acrobats, coffee

cultivation, San Francisco streets, bird flight:
these are some other examples of
Muybridge photographs. Smithson's
sculpture, once under water, is back.
You can walk out on top of it. The bacteria

blooms brighter in late summer than now
and none of my photographs will show it.
I walked to the center and back. I walked
between the rings where the water is
white, the color of milk, from the salt.

The bottom felt like broken glass.
No phone, but two bottles of water
from the gift shop where you can find
postcards showing the famous photograph:
Jupiter meeting *No. 119,* the engineers

wearing similar hats, their fingers almost
touching, rising smoke. It is just before
the champagne toasts, the shots around
of whiskey, the sending of the telegraph:
at last the continent connects.

MOLYBDENUM

—where lavender
comes from, also
aluminum,
as in caught on
the roofline the
ladder that is
leaning and there
allowing that
the sky appear
bitten. It is
a byproduct
of copper. Where
a quarry is
in front of long
blank cliff walls, a
panoply of
crane extensions
propped on cement
blocks if you want
to purchase one.
The photographs
I found Sunday—
thick turquoise pools
of uneven
color cordoned
off in sections:
navy, cyan,
azurite, and
cerulean.
Molybdenum
blue is complex,
an oxide dye.
Sometimes I find
these arguments
to which I can't
connect. Dark lines
trail off without

intention. Most
banal the fact
of unconcern
inside the sun.
Molybdenum
adds toughness in
steel and tungsten.
Throughout the town
arboretum
blue oat grass and
wild moonbeam runs.
The mining holes
abandoned now,
between them just
the blank of land.
Crushed and milled pounds
of ore will go
for just one pound
of dust. Rock-blown
are the hillsides.
What glows inside
the photographs—
silver, brittle—
comes from the dust
and multiplies
in random streaks,
chemicals or
as a stream splits
open the earth's
interior
darkness. It seems
strange this wanting
to be convinced
when already
we lean toward
the things we find
most dangerous.

LULLABY ON THE MARSH

Slack at the end of the lasso's loop
               before the wrist is snapped
Shape of the wave underneath the wave
        before the crescent topples over
Pink stain on the sky with night so soon to drop
Finding the focal point
             and then the moment fading away, back out
Having forgotten the palette
Having just looked past
        so slightly obsessed
      not that the scene follows any of the rules
      not that the scene is picturesque
The grass in the marsh looking particularly sharp—
         be gentle, now—
Achilles by now too angry to eat, as you already know
Achilles pacing by the ships while the men feast—a weight, nothing slack—
The tips of the grass turned by an invisible wind
Prayer that the arrow stay in the house marked North
Prayer that the arrow not flip, not detach, not backward glance—
         be gentle—be good to yourself—
With no one rushing in to interrupt
With no good math for finding a middle
The weight of the moment as felt in the straddle where vectors converge
           where the shallow water will still not collapse
And men who have pulled in the eelgrass to insulate their houses
And men who have pulled the thatch grass to mulch their summer beds
That now the haystacks have become backdrops for the deep dusk-light
      where men have raked the hay, cocked the hay into piles
Having worked a slow careening with the long poles
          as if manipulating the order of the scene
All of this as if epiphany were not a question—
      middle-world, dreamscape
         soft voice kept soft—

Knowing the men will carry the haystacks on gundalows
Knowing in winter across the ice on sleds
Imagining the makeshift roofs shielding the loose tops
                the men tearing across the ice burning rope in their hands
Moment in which Achilles still is stewing, Achilles refusing and refusing to eat
Moment you already know: Achilles and the ambrosia
        so again fate might be complete—look steadily—
Moment before the action takes place
Elsewhere light on the edge of a marsh hawk wing
Not a sound, not even a tick
The water's heavy edge not leaving one mark
Always the moment afterward when the painting is done
The painting propped there, flat
Wordless notes at the hymn end before beginning the next verse
        the fade-out, the unusual shade at dusk—
                                        be gentle—

Years pass—
Blue and low the whole of the world almost seeps
Sit back—
            stop thinking—
Find some other way to coax yourself
There is slack in the loop and a wave in the wave
Tonight the risen moon, pale blank sunk deep in the sky
Keeps on promising sleep

Acknowledgments

I am grateful to the editors of the following publications, in which these poems first appeared: *A Public Space; Black Clock; Beltway Poetry; Colorado Review; Forklift, Ohio; Gulf Coast; Interim; Literary Imagination; Missouri Review Online; Tusculum Review*. "What is Nothing But a Picture" was published as part of the chapbook series *Free Poetry;* thank you to Martin Corless-Smith for his investment in this project.

The poems "Providence" and "For Example" appear in *Topograph: New Writing from the Carolinas and the Landscape Beyond* (Novello Festival Press), edited by Jeff Jackson. I thank G. C. Waldrep and Joshua Corey for their work editing *The Arcadia Project: North American Postmodern Pastoral* (Ahsahta Press) and for including "The Action of a Man."

My colleagues at George Mason University, the generous support of the Mathy Junior Faculty Award and Faculty Research and Development Awards, as well as fellowships from the Virginia Center for the Creative Arts, the Ucross Foundation, Brown Foundation's Dora Maar House, and Fundación Valparaiso, have all provided the time and spirit in which to write. I am very grateful to Daniel Slager at Milkweed Editions, along with Allison Wigen, Kate Strickland, and Wayne Miller. For encouragement and advice, I thank my friends, in particular Dan Beachy-Quick, Srikanth Reddy, Suzanne Buffam, Claudia Rankine, Jen Daniels, and Jim Longenbach.

Sally Keith is the author of two previous collections of poetry, *Dwelling Song* and *Design*. She teaches at George Mason University and lives in Washington, DC.

Milkweed Editions

Founded as a nonprofit organization in 1980, Milkweed Editions is an independent publisher. Our mission is to identify, nurture and publish transformative literature, and build an engaged community around it.

Join Us

In addition to revenue generated by the sales of books we publish, Milkweed Editions depends on the generosity of institutions and individuals like you. In an increasingly consolidated and bottom-line-driven publishing world, your support allows us to select and publish books on the basis of their literary quality and transformative potential. Please visit our Web site (www.milkweed.org) or contact us at (800) 520-6455 to learn more.

Milkweed Editions, a nonprofit publisher, gratefully acknowledges sustaining support from the following:

Maurice and Sally Blanks
Emilie and Henry Buchwald
The Bush Foundation
The Patrick and Aimee Butler
    Foundation
Timothy and Tara Clark
Betsy and Edward Cussler
The Dougherty Family
    Foundation
Mary Lee Dayton
Julie B. DuBois
Joanne and John Gordon
Ellen Grace
William and Jeanne Grandy
Moira Grosbard
John and Andrea Gulla
Elizabeth Driscoll Hlavka and
    Edwin Hlavka
The Jerome Foundation
The Lerner Foundation
The Lindquist & Vennum
    Foundation
Sanders and Tasha Marvin
Robert E. and Vivian McDonald
The McKnight Foundation
Mid-Continent Engineering
The Minnesota State Arts
    Board, through an
    appropriation by the
    Minnesota State Legislature
    and a grant from the National
    Endowment for the Arts
Christine and John L. Morrison
Kelly Morrison and John
    Willoughby

The National Endowment for
    the Arts
Ann and Doug Ness
Jörg and Angie Pierach
The RBC Foundation USA
Deborah Reynolds
Cheryl Ryland
Schele and Philip Smith
The Target Foundation
Edward and Jenny Wahl

ART WORKS.
arts.gov

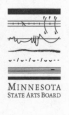

CLEAN WATER LAND & LEGACY AMENDMENT

MINNESOTA
STATE ARTS BOARD

BUSH FOUNDATION

TARGET.

Interior design and typesetting by Hopkins/Baumann
Typeset in Bodoni Book
Printed on acid-free 100% postconsumer waste paper
by Friesens Corporation

 ENVIRONMENTAL BENEFITS STATEMENT

Milkweed Editions saved the following resources by printing the pages of this book on chlorine free paper made with 100% post-consumer waste.

TREES	WATER	ENERGY	SOLID WASTE	GREENHOUSE GASES
8	3,871	3	259	713
FULLY GROWN	GALLONS	MILLION BTUs	POUNDS	POUNDS

 Environmental impact estimates were made using the Environmental Paper Network Paper Calculator. For more information visit www.papercalculator.org.